Facebook for E-Commerce and Business

Facebook for E-Commerce and Business

by Kevin David

Copyright © 2019 by Softiservellc, All rights reserved. Published in United States of America. No part of this publication may be reproduced, distributed, or transmitted in any form or by any means, including photocopying, recording, or other electronic or mechanical methods, without the prior written permission of the author, except in the case of brief quotations embodied in reviews and certain other non-commercial uses permitted by copyright law.

Facebook for E-Commerce and Business has provided the most accurate information possible.

Soft iServe, LLC of Arlington, VA

Softiservellc.com

Book Description

What would you do with 500 leads per month?

Businesses that master the use of social media marketing and connecting are not only gaining huge rewards. They are also building one of their most treasured assets that is loyal customers. Whether you are a start-up founder or a small business owner, naturally, you must use social media platforms to grow your business.

One of the main platforms that initiated innovative marketing techniques for businesses is Facebook. This platform can help you discover new customers, encourage brand loyalty, and turn awareness into sales.

Facebook for Business is a short guidebook that will facilitate success in using Facebook marketing. For starters, this platform comes with a minimum cost, if not free, to share posts, pictures, videos, and encourage them to engage with their customers.

Moreover, this guide will help you build an audience to obtain a higher return on investment. Moreover, there are explained techniques which tend to show the reader the exact strategies to take to achieve business success and generate large volume of leads.

What will you learn from this book?

- Why must you use Facebook for business?
- Essential elements needed to get started
- Establishing campaign goals
- Building a Facebook audience
- Why content is becoming imperative
- Advertising in marketplace
- Utilizing Facebook Insights
- The most common mistakes and how to avoid them.
- And much more!!

Contents

INTRODUCTION 1

CHAPTER 1: WHY DO YOU NEED FACEBOOK FOR YOUR BUSINESS? 3

    LEARN ABOUT YOUR TARGET AUDIENCE 3
    HUMANIZE YOUR COMPANY 4
    GATHER MORE LEADS 4
    BUILD A COMMUNITY 5
    BEAT YOUR COMPETITION 5
    BUILD BRAND LOYALTY 5
    REPUTATION MANAGEMENT 6
    SEO 6
    FACEBOOK ADS 6

CHAPTER 2: GETTING STARTED ON FACEBOOK 7

    STEP 1: SIGN UP 7
    STEP 2: PICK THE RIGHT PROFILE PICTURE AND COVER PHOTO 7
    STEP 3: UPDATE A SHORT DESCRIPTION IN THE "ABOUT" SECTION 8
    STEP 4: PROVIDE BASIC INFORMATION 8
    STEP 5: CREATE YOUR FIRST POST 9
    STEP 6: CONNECT YOUR TOUCH POINTS 9
    STEP 7: CONNECT WITH OTHER BUSINESSES 9
    STEP 8: KEEP ENGAGING! 10
    STEP 9: SET ACHIEVABLE GOALS 10

CHAPTER 3: HOW TO SET YOUR FACEBOOK BUSINESS CAMPAIGN GOALS 11

    FACEBOOK CLUSTERS THEIR AIMS INTO THREE PARTS OF THE FUNNEL: 11
        Awareness 11
        Brand Awareness 11
        Reach 11
    CONSIDERATION 11
        Traffic 12
        Engagement 12
        App Installs 12
        Video Views 12
        Lead Generation 13
    CONVERSION 13
        Product Catalog Sales 14
        Store Visits 14

CHAPTER 4: HOW TO BUILD YOUR AUDIENCE ON FACEBOOK 15

    SIZE OF YOUR TARGET AUDIENCE 15
    TYPES OF FACEBOOK AUDIENCES 15
        Saved audience 15
        Custom audience 16

- *Lookalike audience* 16

CHAPTER 5: CONTENT IS KING ON FACEBOOK 18
- THE BACKBONE OF SEARCH ENGINE OPTIMIZATION 18
- ENCOURAGES ENGAGEMENT 18
- BECOME A THOUGHT LEADER IN YOUR INDUSTRY 19
- INITIATES AND MAINTAINS LOYALTY 19
- QUALITY CONTENT INCREASES WEBSITE TRAFFIC 19

CHAPTER 6: ENHANCING YOUR FACEBOOK PAGE WITH APPLICATIONS 21
- CANVA 21
- HOOTSUITE 21
- SURVEYMONKEY 21
- BIGCOMMERCE 22
- FACEBOOK PIXEL 22
- LIKEALYZER 22
- MOBILEMONKEY 23

CHAPTER 7: HOW TO ADVERTISE IN THE FACEBOOK MARKETPLACE 24
- CREATE AN AD CAMPAIGN WITH APPLICABLE OBJECTIVE 24
- CREATE A NEW AD SET 24
- PICK THE MARKETPLACE AD PLACEMENT 24
- CREATE A FACEBOOK MARKETPLACE VIDEO AD 25
- ANALYZE MARKETPLACE AD PLACEMENT OUTCOMES 25

CHAPTER 8: 8 COMMON FACEBOOK MARKETING MISTAKES (AND HOW TO AVOID THEM) 26
- TOO FOCUSED ON SELLING 26
- BEGGING FOR LIKES 26
- IGNORING NEGATIVE FEEDBACK 27
- NOT PAYING TO PLAY 27
- POSTING BORING OR OFF-BRAND CONTENT 27
- PUBLISHING THE WRONG TYPE OF CONTENT 28
- NOT MAKING THE MOST OF FACEBOOK'S AD OPTIONS 28
- REFUSING TO EVOLVE WITH FACEBOOK'S ALGORITHM 28

CONCLUSION 30

Introduction

Started in Feb 2004, Facebook is one of the most leading platforms among the highly utilized social networking websites. It is a social website that allows users to develop a free of cost account. Facebook is a user-friendly platform that is open to everybody. It can be utilized by all individuals even if they are not pros in the technological areas. Anyone can simply create an account and start posting.

Even though it started out as a way to keep in touch or reconnect with long-lost friends, it quickly became the best tool for businesses. Not only does this platform assist organizations to monitor their target audience closely, but it also delivers ads to individuals who just need a nudge to purchase the services or products.

Moreover, businesses can obtain access to personal profiles. The major benefit of having access to these profiles is that businesses can get in-depth insights, understand behavior patterns, and it facilitates businesses to engage with their esteemed customers.

When starting out on Facebook, the majority of people are not clear on certain concepts. But before investing money, you must be able to differentiate between profiles and pages. Simply put, a personal profile is for individuals who want to keep it private and post their stuff. On the contrary, a page is for companies.

With a profile, users will have to put in a request to be your friend or to enter in the friend list. You will have the authority of accepting or rejecting the request, which will ensure whether or not someone can view your content. Profiles have features such as Chat and gaming abilities that are not accessible to Pages. To make a profile, you have to sign up on Facebook from its home page with a private email address, inserting your personal info, not the data of your company.

A Page, conversely, necessitates a user to "follow or like, "which allows them to access the content. The page's content will then become visible on the newsfeed. These pages are generally created based on a cause, for an organization to market their products or services, or it could be for getting jobs. Pages are different and can be formed from a current account, and more than one person can be assigned to act as admin. You can also create a Page through your Profile.

If your aim is to market your product or increase business reach, then you must craft a Page. It should initiate from the individual who will have the main access to it. To make a Page, log on to your profile and press "Like Pages." It will show you Create Page options, and this platform will guide you on the rest of the process. Facebook also allows you to edit settings.

You must opt for someone who you can trust and who is linked with your brand. Give them the role of a manager so that they become accountable formally.

Next, you must add in top-notch content to your page. Putting in your contact information is imperative such as email address, telephone number, or a link to the website. Moreover, the "About" section should be up-to-date. This will give a brief description of the company which consumers appreciate all the time.

Chapter 1: Why Do You Need Facebook for Your Business?

In this technologically advanced era, social media has seeped in the lives of most individuals in the world. As customers, people spend more than 2 hours on social media per day. Facebook is presently the most utilized social media platform. Regarding monthly active users and reach, this platform had roughly 2.27 billion monthly active users last year. This is about one-third of the total world population. So, it will not be that silly to state that businesses can reach an enormous consumer base using Facebook. I talk more deeply about this concept in my course https://softiservellc.com/product/kevin-david-facebook-ads-course/.

This platform offers a distinct marketing opportunity for businesses by creating Facebook Business Pages. With more people exploring social media, these sites have become some of the main online sources they utilize to find out more about organizations, products, artists, and the latest world events. Facebook Marketing has a viral outcome – that is, information spreads via social networks exponentially.

Creating a Facebook business page can aid a business to connect and reach their existing and prospective consumer base. Presently, there are more than 50 million Business pages on Facebook because people's buying decision is based on social media. There are two key methods for companies to promote on Facebook.

The first is through using Facebook Pages, and the second is from Facebook Groups. Groups tend to be focused on getting together groups of individuals who share mutual interests, while pages are medium where users can network around a specific brand or product. Given that businesses utilize Facebook Pages, we will focus on reasons as to why it is important.

Learn About Your Target Audience

A company page on Facebook offers you a means to communicate straight and openly with your target audience. This is a lot similar to an ongoing focus group where you can obtain in-depth knowledge about your customer base. People who like the page are mostly those who have some information about your company and are eager to learn more. While they definitely are expecting to collect valuable information from your page, you also can be gathering beneficial data from the customers through their engagement.

Facebook Insights also delivers handy information about your customers and their exchanges on your page. As a representative group of your target market, the fans on Facebook can give away a lot through their comments, interaction, and feedback.

Target audience is a huge subject and I covered it in details in a full video here: https://softiservellc.com/product/kevin-david-facebook-ads-course/.

Humanize Your Company

Integral parts of social media include genuine communication and social connections. Facebook offers you a chance to assign a name, face, and personality to your brand. Though your Facebook page might characterize your company, it also lets you demonstrate the human side of your organization through personal conversations and non-business interaction. This is even true if you automate your social media activity. The platform comes with a wide variety of tools that allow you to fit in a reasonable amount of live, real-time communication. As a result, relationships become richer and more human-like.

Gather More Leads

Although Facebook allows you to connect with people (who like your page), this just isn't enough. It is imperative that you build long term sustainable relationships with your customers. What if Facebook disappears one day? It is this relationship that will help you go on and keep increasing your business. Smart business owners aim to accumulate leads in the form of email addresses.

This way, you can stay in touch with your customers outside the Facebook platform, as well. You can send your fans updated about giveaways, contests, and even the monthly newsletter. But it is crucial to have a presence on Facebook because this is the primary source through which you can get those leads in the first place.

Generating leads from Facebook is a step-by-step process which I explained thoroughly in my course https://softiservellc.com/product/kevin-david-facebook-ads-course/.

Build a Community

Facebook pages are an outstanding channel to collect your existing customers and prospects to share opinions, give away reviews, voice issues, and offer a reaction. There is a number of ways through which you can build a community on Facebook, such as:

- Posting valuable, pertinent and stimulating links
- Requesting loyal customers to add with comments
- Initiating contests and promotions
- Offering inducements for action on the page

It is significant for businesses to have a Facebook page because it permits them to develop a loyal following that will persist in growing.

Beat your competition

Indulging in an activity simply because your opposition is doing it is just not a good enough reason, however when it comes to social networks such as Facebook, not having a presence online or an updated page can cost you big time.

In this cut-throat environment, not having a Facebook page can cost you major opportunities. Naturally, this will hinder the growth of the company. Being on Facebook becomes essential if your competition already exists on the platform and also doing well.

Build Brand Loyalty

In addition to being a place where you can sell products and build a customer base, a business page on Facebook can do marvels for facilitating you to shape brand loyalty. If you constantly deliver valuable and amusing content, your fans will remain loyal -- even when you make errors. These days, individuals search online to find companies to purchase from -- and they mainly search social media.

When your followers perceive you as being responsive, they are more likely to carry out transactions with you compared to a company that has no Facebook presence or a below-par page activity.

If brand loyalty is what you aim for, Facebook allows you to do this seamlessly. Refer to more resources here: https://softiservellc.com/product/kevin-david-facebook-ads-course/.

Reputation Management
Facebook lets a company obtain a profound understanding of how the brand is observed online – via direct feedback. Moreover, they can also track what customers are saying about the brand. As a consequence, you can alter your branding strategies to improve the image and reputation. This will eventually impact the ROI of a business.

SEO
Search Engine Optimization is a crucial feature for anybody who wants to shape a noteworthy presence on the web. Having a page on Facebook for your business can assist you in your SEO struggles, as well. Mostly, all the posts and links on the page are considered by search engines. So if you are looking for a jump in the SEO rankings, then constantly update relevant content on your page.

Facebook Ads
Your business at Facebook is not merely restricted to a fan page or a group. The platform offers you an opportunity to place ad campaigns as well. You can create your advertisements, and as per your budget necessities, opt for a campaign appropriate for your business needs. In addition, you can also select the people you want to target and who will view these particular ads. You can set the criteria and adjust numerous variables. Targeting can be done based on educational level, demographics, and interests, etc. It is up to you to determine how frequently these ads will appear.

Facebook loves advertisers. It's a win-win situation for businesses. I talk in more details about this in my course https://softiservellc.com/product/kevin-david-facebook-ads-course/.

Chapter 2: Getting Started On Facebook

Once you have figured out why you MUST have a Facebook Page for your business, it is time to move on to the next step. Entering the platform and having a strong page can be a challenge. While so many businesses already have a strong existence on Facebook, numerous others are trying to start off on the right foot. This chapter of the book gives a step-by-step guide to getting started on Facebook and establishing a name in the social sphere.

To be successful on social media, you must have a one-stop destination for customers that can assist them in searching you online. Definitely, for this, you have to have a Facebook Business Page. Some of the important steps to take before certifying that you have an engaged and active audience are:

Step 1: Sign up

This is a simple step, and you may know it already. Just go to facebook.com/business and press on the Create a Page button at the top. The first thing you will have to do when crafting your Page is to select the right "sort" for your company. There are six choices, but most small organizations tend to choose from "Company, Organization, or Institution" or "Local Business or Place."

If your business style falls into different categories, then you can select the one in which the majority of your customers are likely to consider you. When you press on a business category, a box will show up asking for a few additional details, such as the name of your organization, your address, and your Page type. Categories are essentially sub-groups within the bigger business category you have previously selected. When you begin typing in the category field, you will see a list of possible category alternatives to opt from.

Step 2: Pick the right profile picture and cover photo

One of the top reasons for Facebook being a great marketing tool is that it allows an organization to demonstrate a story visually. When it comes to creating your Page, there are two key components; your cover photo and your profile picture.

While uploading these two pictures, you must be wise about it because they will create a visual impact. Ensure the photos you select align with your business and are easily recognizable in this cluttered marketplace.

Uploading profile pictures come first. The profile picture accompanies your organization's name in search results and even when you interrelate with users. It also shows on the top left of your Page. If you are a famous business, then it is advised that you upload a picture of your logo. For a local business, a good option is to apply a well-shot image of the signature product or offer. This will show the follower or fans to get connected quickly.

The profile picture will become visible as a square on the Facebook Page. However, it will be cut out in a circle when in ads and posts. So it is essential that you don't place any vital details there. Click Upload picture, and you are good to go.

When people first visit your page, they will view the cover photo first. This has a massive impact on the first impression. The purpose is to aid small businesses in improving the way they tell a story rather than giving additional space to sell their product. Never clutter your cover photo with a lot of promotional content. Instead, select an image that encapsulates your business and appeals to potential fans.

Step 3: Update a Short Description in the "About" Section
When people look up your page on Facebook, they must be able to find out the information they are searching for in the "About" section. This incorporates your company's overview, mission, and a short description. It gives you a chance to introduce the business to your potential followers and present them with information that tells who you are exactly. Moreover, give them an excellent reason to "Like" the page.

Step 4: Provide Basic Information
The biggest advantage for small businesses is the amount of data that they are allowed to share on this platform. In the "about" section, apart from writing an engaging description, a brand can also add specific details that are imperative. Small businesses can fill out details such as payment methods that are accepted, hours of operation,

parking availability near your office, etc. In addition, Facebook allows you to modify the fields according to the category of your business, industry-related, and the services you offer.

Step 5: Create your first post
It is a better idea to develop valuable posts prior to inviting the audience to your page. You can either produce some of your own posts or update pertinent content from opinion leaders within the industry. It is advised that the first post should be a mixture of rich media and text.

You must create a post that not only helps people to familiarize themselves with the brand but also encourage them to interact with it and also spread positive word of mouth. Be creative so that visitors are tempted to stick around on the page once they visit it. Your Facebook Business Page now signifies a vigorous online presence that will make prospective consumers and fans to feel comfortable networking with you.

Step 6: Connect your touch points
Building a following is difficult, particularly when you are beginning from scratch. However, if somebody already joined your email list, they will definitely love to connect with you on Facebook. Deliver an email to the people in your contact list and invite them to "Like" your Facebook page. Once they do so, it will automatically display new posts on their feed, which assists in engaging.

Step 7: Connect with other businesses
When getting started on Facebook, it may seem intimidating that other businesses are receiving such extraordinary results when it comes to attracting a fan base and engaging their followers. Nonetheless, all organizations, no matter where they are in terms of followers, had to begin at some point. To create your own success, you might want to use their experience. Moreover, you can also observe the type of content which is liked by the customers. You can also link with other local Pages and initiate the building of a beneficial support group in the community.

Step 8: Keep engaging!
Publishing a page on Facebook is not enough to be successful. When getting started with this platform, it is essential to have a consistent activity. You won't be able to accomplish actual results if you only post when there is something noteworthy or just once per month. You must post regularly but ensure that you are not over-posting. If you update more than 1-2 status updates in a day, fans might get annoyed and un-like the Page.

Step 9: Set achievable goals
When getting started, do not get overpowered by setting unattainable goals. Rather than this, you can concentrate on providing valued content to your customers and followers while paying attention to the way they are engaging.

Chapter 3: How to Set Your Facebook Business Campaign Goals

The objectives of a Facebook ad are the main support of any campaign. This is because these goals tend to regulate the bidding options, the way a campaign will be optimized, and also your ad unit options. There are numerous campaign objectives to select from, which can be overwhelming. Your campaign goals essentially tell this platform what it is that you aspire to accomplish, and the algorithm will offer you the paramount tools to do it. Walk over my shoulders in my course https://softiservellc.com/product/kevin-david-facebook-ads-course/ and see how I do it live.

Facebook clusters their aims into three parts of the funnel:

Awareness
These objectives come at the top of funnel to produce interest in your offerings. For awareness, you can focus on two basic objectives:

Brand Awareness
This campaign goal is utilized when the brand is only looking to augment awareness of their business rather than wanting their followers to engage with the content. They may not even want to click through, purchases, or opt-ins. It will aid you in reaching out to individuals who are more expected to be attentive to the message in the ad. The goal will be beneficial for bigger organizations that intend to put the brand on top of the consumers' minds. If you have a smaller enterprise, this may not be for you.

Reach
Utilize the Reach goal to ensure that more people within the target audience view your ad while still adhering to the budget constraints. This objective can facilitate to target a smaller audience. It is employed when the priority is to reach more individuals within the audience as possible.

Consideration
This objective considers utilizing these to reach individuals with some interest in what you are offering and who might want to learn more. You can try one of the following objectives then:

Traffic
When you intend to drive traffic from outside Facebook, then you can employ this objective. It could get more people to read your blog, visit the landing page, listen to your podcast, or even to use your app. Facebook will display your ad to those individuals inside the target audience who are likely to press on your link, contingent upon their previous behaviors.

Engagement
Ultimately every marketer on Facebook wants its customers to engage with their content. If you are at that stage, then using the engagement objective is a smart move. This is where a marketer intends that their ads will receive likes, reactions, shares, and comments. You can also use this particular goal if you want to produce more Offer Claims, Page Likes, or Event Responses.

If you optimize this objective for your campaign, it implies that Facebook is conveying your advertisement to individuals who will interact with it. This will eventually increase reach, and you will receive organic reach in the news feed beyond what you paid for.

App Installs
You can also employ the App Installs aim if you have an app and want to redirect individuals to the store where they can install the app.

Video Views
You can apply the Video Views objective when you are endorsing a video, and your main aim is to get more individuals to see your video. This is even beneficial if your priority is not that these people click on the link. Video Views is an amazing goal to select when

you intend to create a video engagement audience for retargeting dedications in future campaigns.

Lead Generation

This is an excellent objective that can be utilized when a brand is only looking to generate leads on Facebook within the ad. It is also useful when you do not want to drive traffic to another site. Lead Generation ads let you acquire information like name, phone number, and email ID, etc. Moreover, there is an auto-populating feature now, which makes it easier for individuals to complete the lead form.

As a result, you receive the best information as the majority of individuals utilize their email addresses to log in to Facebook. When you use Lead Ads, you fundamentally require a third-party tool that assimilates with Facebook and robotically gets the emails you are netting via your Lead Ads. It then places them into CRM or the email marketing software you are making use of to convey the offer you are endorsing.

One of the disadvantages of utilizing the Lead Generation goal is that you will not be creating your website traffic audience as a consequence of the receiving lead experience because individuals will not have to opt-in to visit the website.

This is my favorite way when it comes to Facebook ads, which I talked about it in my course https://softiservellc.com/product/kevin-david-facebook-ads-course/

Conversion

Conversion goals come towards the bottom of the funnel and must be utilized when you want individuals to download, register, opt-in, buy, or visit the store. Simply put, it is essential to utilize this as a campaign goal when you wish that people convert for a particular action.

It is imperative that you get a minimum of 15-25 conversions in a week if you are looking to optimize it. This smallest number of conversions offers Facebook with adequate information to be able to study about those individuals that transform. It will also make expectations around those individuals who are more expected to convert from the target audience and then distribute the ads to more of those people.

A bare minimum is 15-25 conversions, while an ideal amount is 50-100+. The higher the conversions, the better it is because Facebook will acquire more data to work with.

Product Catalog Sales

When you own an e-commerce store, it is essential that you utilize the Product Catalog goal. It is also beneficial when you would want to endorse products from your catalog. This necessitates you to integrate the product catalog with Facebook and create feeds that you can select from when producing your campaigns.

Store Visits

If you wish to promote your business while having multiple locations, then you can use the Store Visits Facebook ad objective. You will have to systemize your business locations in the business manager beforehand in order to employ this goal. It can present as an excellent method to capture foot traffic for the business. Moreover, it can convey ads which are based on an individual's current location.

In the end, the aim of any campaign is to optimize ad delivery. This can only be achieved when you select suitable objectives for every campaign.

Chapter 4: How to Build Your Audience on Facebook

Whether it is to stay connected with your existing followers or getting in touch with prospective fans, Facebook is the best platform for it. This platform houses over two billion individuals, so there is a high chance that your particular audience being present here. To reach these customers in an efficient manner, you can utilize Facebook ads. However, to run an ad, comprising of the boosting posts feature, you must set up a Facebook Audience.

Building a Facebook audience is not rocket science; nevertheless, with the apparently never-ending waves of targeting alternatives accessible, it sure can feel like it. Let's look at the process of developing an Audience on Facebook.

Three types of audiences will be discussed below, but for every one of them, you will have the same initial process. Go to your Facebook account and then open the business manager. When you click on the three-line menu extension, it will provide all alternatives. You will then enter a new page, where you can click "Create Audience."

Size of your Target Audience

The size of your audience is way more imperative, then you think. It is easy to be mistaken in the first stage by selecting a very narrow audience. Smaller the target audience, the higher the odds of strong competition ensuing higher Cost per thousand impressions. A constricted audience will also result in under-delivery of the ad. So you must be able to get the right audience while certifying that the group isn't too small. You may also want to use the Facebook algorithm. It is designed to narrow the audience contingent upon your objectives of the campaign.

Types of Facebook Audiences

Naturally, you need to understand the diverse types of Facebook audience that you can create for ad purposes.

Saved audience

The type of audience you will select to create one on Facebook will be dependent on your goal. If you are looking to find new customers who have never visited your page before, then you can utilize the "Saved Audience" option. This kind of audience is made by choosing the demographics and interests of individuals on Facebook. This is why it is so crucial to have your consumer personas because, without it, you will not have the data essential to create these saved audiences.

For this, you must turn to the audience in the AD manager, then choose "create audience" and click on "saved audience." Subsequent to this, you can select particular interests and characteristics to define groups that will like the product. You will have to opt for a location but ensure that it is not too broad, for instance, the entire country. Knowing your clients geographically will decrease wasted ad expenditure. After choosing the location, you can keep narrowing down dependent on gender, age, and even language.

Custom audience
Custom audience groups are essential for a business because it is built to target individuals who have engaged with your business before. You can find the user contingent upon your site's visitor URL or import the existing customer's list. You can also build custom audience clusters based on Facebook interaction or app activity. There are presently five methods of building a custom audience: customer file, app activity, website traffic, offline activity, and engagement.

The customer file is normally created off an email list. It can either be done by uploading a saved email list or through MailChimp. This can incorporate information such as birthday, city, name, zip code, etc. The more information you have, the narrower your audience will be. Moreover, you can utilize Facebook Pixel to monitor individuals who have interacted with your page. Then you can build an audience based on the amount spent on the page or people who have visited specific pages etc.

Lookalike audience

A lookalike audience is new potential customers that Facebook spontaneously builds reliant on existing audiences. This is excellent for acquiring new customers, similar to your present customers. You can develop a lookalike audience dependent on individuals in one of your custom audiences or of individuals who want to interact with your page.

Simply select the page or audience and the location you want to target. Then you can pick the size of your Facebook audience. Although it might be appealing to decide on the largest audience size, however, the larger you go, your present audience won't lookalike. You have to select from a range of 1-10. Try and opt from 1-3 so that the audience looks a lot like you selected.

Watch me how I choose the target audience, and how I create a custom and lookalike audiences live in my course https://softiservellc.com/product/kevin-david-facebook-ads-course/

Chapter 5: Content is king on Facebook

When it comes to Facebook marketing, "likes" are just like consuming empty calories. Real power is in the content. For the past few years, the content has totally controlled the online world of business. Brands try hard to engage with their customers in several different ways, and developing high-quality content through a diverse medium is the method of capturing their attention.

Content comes in numerous forms; you might post high-value visuals on social media sites or share blog posts. In an effort to reach your audience, brands might even create live video streams or podcasts. On Facebook, content is king and is expected to stay this way for a number of reasons, including:

The backbone of Search Engine Optimization

If you want your website to achieve a high ranking in the search engine, then it is essential for you to post valuable content on the website. Without good content, Google will have nothing to rank your site in the search engine. When the content has good quality, it will attract readers.

Similarly, Google will spot your Off-page and On-page SEO efforts, which will facilitate in improving the rank. When people read it, share it, and eventually engage with the content, the search engines will solidify the rank and keep you on top of the Google page. You may also utilize guest posting because it is an excellent way to get high-value, pertinent links leading to your site.

Encourages engagement

More than likes, a brand should focus on getting a higher level of engagement with their customers. This goal can be achieved easily. Top-quality content, irrespective of the type, will persuade users to participate with the brand without even realizing it. If the content you produce is authentic, users will stop interacting with it and consume the message of the brand. Build a relationship by pushing the content via social media channels and ensure that it is easy to share.

Become a Thought Leader in Your Industry
If the content that you are generating is valued by your audience, you will ultimately be seen as a thought leader for your particular industry. This development will come unsurprisingly after sharing sufficient content that you become someone who can be trusted easily.

Once you establish yourself as a thought leader in your industry, this will naturally generate a buzz in the field. Other strong individuals will also start to approach you for collaboration or request you to write guest blog posts. The key to becoming a thought the leader is sharing high-value content with your potential audience.

Initiates and Maintains Loyalty
As powerful content will lead you to engage with your customers, it won't be difficult to sell your service or product to them. There will be a tremendous amount of loyalty as they consume your content on a consistent basis. Moreover, they will develop a special connection with you through spoken and written words.

Excellent content will lead to a strong connection, and that will lead them to talk about you and spread positive word of mouth in their circle. Apart from this, your loyal customers will also feel good about themselves each time they check your site. It is a natural response because they feel a relationship to you and their devotion to you and your brand makes them pleased to be connected with your company.

Quality Content Increases Website Traffic
When you produce engaging videos, prized informational blog posts, and remarkable audio interviews and post them all over your Facebook page, it will also lead you to direct traffic to your website. By focusing on diverse content types, you will be able to appeal to a bigger and wider audience who will interact on social media pages, websites, and blogs.

You must remember that everyone is not equal, and people will appreciate different content types across dissimilar mediums. When you share good content on all medium, it will lead to form a healthy audience of prospective consumers that would come back for more information.

Chapter 6: Enhancing Your Facebook Page with Applications

There are more than 80 million SME's pages on Facebook, a figure that is increasing by the year. If you want your business page on Facebook to stand out in this crowded marketplace, then enhance it with apps. Today you will find an application for almost anything. Numerous apps can facilitate Facebook managers to augment the user's involvement significantly.

The idea is to keep the customers engaged and craving to come back for more. When you are able to do so, there are higher chances for "viral visibility."In short, every time a fan engages with your Facebook page, it is similar to free advertising for you since the activity will be displayed in their News Feed. Here are some of the best apps that you must use:

Canva

If you do not have access to a graphic designer, then Canva is your best friend. It offers more than 50,000 templates for all sorts of things from page cover photos to posts. Every template can be personalized, permitting you to upload logos and images to generate collages and add branding elements. In addition, you do not have to worry about licensing and sourcing stock pictures.

Hootsuite

Hootsuite's scheduling choice sallow you to post at the perfect times of the day and place campaigns beforehand. As a business, you can add to your Facebook page or numerous social networks at one time without the hassle. Apart from saving time, scheduling permits your page to remain active outside the conventional 9-5 work hours. Hootsuite lets you elect team leaders to validate posts, ensuring they are on-message and on-brand.

SurveyMonkey

Brands might opt to run a poll for a range of reasons, from enhancing engagement levels or conducting market research. SurveyMonkey provides free and professional tools to generate polls or surveys precisely for your page on Facebook. Using this, you can produce your own survey or create it on the basis of a template. You will receive tips while creating the polls, and the results will be delivered in real-time. By means of Survey Monkey Audience, you can also reach a specific group, augmenting your chances of getting results from the right people. Moreover, it will also offer Facebook Messenger surveys, making it easier to get them done through Messenger.

BigCommerce

If your Facebook page also acts as a retail platform, then you must consider using BigCommerce. Like Shopify, BigCommerce is an approved app for e-commerce. It facilitates the brand to run a store from their Facebook page. Through this app, brands can run targeted ads, associate their website catalog, and discover the right customers.

Facebook Pixel

Facebook Pixel is precisely an analytics app. Nevertheless, it is needed to ensure you can monitor and target your ads. With this app, you can link with particular types of customers, arrange automatic bidding, and better comprehend the customer purchasing path. If you are delivering ads without Pixel, you will be missing out on Facebook's full abilities.

Likealyzer

Likealyzer employs data points to deliver a grade and comprehensive report card for your Facebook Page performance. Subsequently, Likealyzer will also breakdown at points where your company's Facebook page is excelling and where it needs improvement. It will robotically classify competitors for you to mark against. However, you can also physically add them as well.

MobileMonkey

MobileMonkey is an app that offers more than one purpose for Messenger on Facebook. It aids in building chatbots, sends chat blasts, produces Messenger ads, and even provides tools for growing Messenger lists. If you are already using Hootsuite, you can combine it with your dashboard, so it becomes easy for you to restructure marketing tasks and Messenger response.

When you integrate these apps with your Facebook page, you will be able to manage it better and enhance the activity by constantly improving the strategy.

Chapter 7: How to Advertise In the Facebook Marketplace

Facebook Marketplace is one of the biggest individual-to-individual selling platforms accessible online. It is an open exchange where people can purchase and sell new and pre-owned objects to other people. Today, Facebook is huge enough that a business must not ignore it, especially after its expansion in Marketplace Ads.

When you promote utilizing the Marketplace placement, you are not endorsing a product that you are trying to sell. Rather, you are marketing in the same way you will in the news feed or the other engagement alternatives. This chapter focuses on a step-by-step guide to advertising on this marketplace.

Create an Ad Campaign with Applicable Objective

The marketplace is accessible as a placement opportunity merely for specific campaign goals. For now, it can be utilized with the Traffic, Reach, Video Views, Conversions, and Catalogue Sales objectives. If a business already has a campaign with one of these objectives, then they can skip this step. Otherwise, you can move to the Ad Manager and press on "Create."Then you must choose appropriate campaign objectives. After that, you must assign a name to the campaign.

Create a New Ad Set

You will select a site as to where a business manager wants to drive traffic to. Like other ads, you need to select your audience and also describe them by age, location, gender, connection, and language. Then scroll down to placements. Your ad set can incorporate the audience, budget, placements, and traffic, etc.

Pick the Marketplace Ad Placement

Facebook's Marketplace is presently coming out as the latest ad placement. It is not yet accessible worldwide. If you want to see whether the feature is obtainable in your country, you can easily scroll down to the Placements segment. You will notice that in its default setting, Facebook has checked to market on all placements. Then you can choose

Edit Placements. For ad accounts that can utilize this feature, the Marketplace is incorporated when Automatic Placements is chosen. It implies that several Facebook marketers will be advertising in the Marketplace without recognizing it.

Create a Facebook Marketplace Video Ad

You can move on to the Ad Creation segment. The suggested ad specifications for Marketplace are similar to the ones in the Newsfeed. You will not be able to modify the ad creative among the two placements. Although the ads might look similar to both placements, the setting will be different, and some things will work better in the Marketplace. For instance, the Marketplace is controlled by stationary images, so videos predominantly demonstrations of the products will stick out.

Analyze Marketplace Ad Placement Outcomes

Similar to other advertising on Facebook, it is recommended that you test out Marketplace placement as well. Its exclusivity implies that this is expected to deliver pronounced results for specific products, businesses, and ad formats. You can filter your ad reports to see a comparison in performance with other placements.

More on this in my course https://softiservellc.com/product/kevin-david-facebook-ads-course/

Chapter 8: 8 Common Facebook Marketing Mistakes (And How to Avoid Them)

Social media is a tremendously powerful medium of engrossing your target audience; however, if used in the wrong way, it can convert to being extremely hazardous for your brand. Just because you have made a business page on Facebook does not imply that there won't be any mistakes. It is not always necessary that mistakes are bad; if you can learn from them, then they can be avoided the next time.

Too Focused On Selling

Although this is an obvious point, sometimes brands tend to focus on selling and promoting their products only. Facebook for brands has to be about generating a community and a conversation that endorses the brand's lifestyle rather than spamming your followers with ads.

The majority of the brands aim to push their products down the user's throats. Today consumers are more equipped with identifying genuine content versus when they are being forced to purchase. As a business, you must try a soft-sell technique that offers genuine content.

Preferably, the 80/20 principle is seen as a good gauge for isolating posts; 80% of your brand's updates must be engaging while the posts that endorse your services and goods must not surpass 20%.

Begging for Likes

Some of the brand's content literally begs for "Likes." The truth is that if you are requesting your customers to like your page or post, they will perceive it as a desperate attempt, and it will show that a proper Facebook marketing strategy is absent. Moreover, such posts are buried by Facebook.

People on this platform want to watch videos that are funny, and that updates them on the latest events in their circle. If a brand is asking for likes, they will either skip it or add some negative comments. You must offer your fans helpful content frequently, and raise "real questions" that trigger engagement. Although getting more likes is a good thing, you must look for brand advocates instead. These are individuals who like your post, share it with their connections, and advertise your business for free.

Ignoring Negative Feedback

When on social media, negative feedback is unavoidable. As a brand, you must not forget that you have a face online and cannot get away with anything you feel like doing. When a brand gets negative feedback, they can fight it, ignore it, or cope with it. Some businesses take a short route and simply delete or ignore negative comments.

Although it may seem an easy way, it is very dangerous. Remember that the customers are constantly watching, and competitors are waiting to take advantage of the mistakes you will make. Rather than turning a blind eye, make the best out of the situation. Respond promptly and thoughtfully to demonstrate that you are dedicated to the highest customer fulfillment.

Not Paying To Play

Even though Facebook is a zero to minimum cost, you will still not be able to reach the maximum potential of marketing without paying. Once you pay, the audience increases, and more people tend to view your content. With excellent content, you will be able to receive good organic reach, but you have to pay for a wider audience. You can utilize the "boost post" feature to get more engagement on your brand instantaneously.

Posting Boring or Off-Brand Content

This may come as a shock, but the things you update on Facebook must be pertinent to your brand. If you are running a company that sells laptop covers, then it does not make sense that you post about a random project only because you think it is cool. When you are on-brand, there is a high chance that you will receive higher engagement.

Remember, just because your followers love your product, they don't have to have the same interests. Given that your followers do not look at all your post sharing irrelevant stuff will only cost you to waste their time. This will incur negative engagement on the post.

Publishing the Wrong Type Of Content

There are different types of content that can work for your brand. It is imperative to choose wisely. If you use unrelated hashtags or mix up trends that are not linked with each other, then you may experience a major blow. Looking to increase the engagement, then updating an unsuitable picture or comment, utilizing clickbait, being all about sales, and traffic will not work.

Moreover, Facebook is putting down click-bait posts and will constantly obscure them in the newsfeed. This is why it is imperative to be creative and original. You can publish BTS pictures of employees, or what happens in a typical day at your company. This will enhance brand engagement, perception, and likes on the page.

Not Making the Most of Facebook's Ad Options

Not every business has an excess budget to spend on Facebook ads. But if you utilize this option, then you will definitely benefit from it. The ad must be obvious and clear as what is being promoted because it makes it easier for the consumers to recall. You might also want to incorporate some sort of "payoff" since advertisements with a reward are likely to be more powerful over buying decisions. The help from the ad tools does not end at the "Boost Post" feature. You can dig deeper into Facebook Insights to generate creative content. Moreover, you can also employ the promoted posts option to extend the reach.

The true potential of Facebook advertising cannot be quantified; brands should take specific steps in creating ads that offer great incentives while achieving business goals. Similarly, you can use Power Editor to gain leads from Facebook.

Refusing to Evolve with Facebook's Algorithm

Facebook modifies its algorithm erratically; the recent alterations in the Facebook algorithm comprise of bringing content to users contingent upon their preceding interaction. It is imperative for businesses to stay updated about the recent updates so that constant user experience and ads can be generated. Brands must bookmark Facebook for pages to remain updated with the newest algorithm and implement to augment brand perception and engagement.

Conclusion

With Facebook housing more than 2 billion people on the platform, it is only smart to have a presence on it. If your business does not engage its customers on Facebook, then you must create a page this instant; otherwise, you will be missing out on an important segment. This book begins by introducing the difference between a profile and a page. As a business, you will have to create a page.

Moving on, the guide explains convincing points for a business to have a Facebook page. Mainly, you need to enhance two-way communication, humanize the company, and build a community of loyal customers. You will then be assisted in getting started on Facebook through a step-by-step guide. Moreover, it acts as a guide to set the business campaign goals.

Having the right audience on this platform is a major milestone that you must achieve. This is why this excellent guide talks about the diverse audience types and how to integrate them in your page. Then it explains the reason you must have excellent content on the Page.

Engagement is the key element. The content, whether it is blogs or videos, must ensure that the customers are hooked to it so that they are willing to come back for more. Furthermore, this book also suggests the use of a variety of applications to make the best of Facebook marketing for businesses.

Not only will these apps guarantee the methodical posting of content, but it will also facilitate you to obtain valuable information to update the strategy consistently. Best of all, the book explains the major mistakes that are made by the majority of marketers. This will help you understand and avoid these at all costs, saving time and money.

I encourage you to go to my course https://softiservellc.com/product/kevin-david-facebook-ads-course/, and don't hesitate to contact me at kevin.david@softiservellc.com if you have any questions.

About the author:

The author helps small businesses and entrepreneurs increase their revenue by 500% on the high end within 90 days, consistently. He does this by lead generation that work. Whatever services and products you are offering, these leads are potential clients who gave permission exclusively to contact them by emails and phone numbers and are interest in what you have to offer. For more information, you may contact the author at info@outechsolutions.com
Or by phone at 571-599-4371

www.ingramcontent.com/pod-product-compliance
Lightning Source LLC
Chambersburg PA
CBHW030547220526
45463CB00007B/3011